Wampum Belts

of the

Iroquois

WAMPUM BELTS

of the

IROQUOIS

by

TEHANETORENS

Book Publishing Company
Summertown, Tennessee

Cover painting by Kahionhes (John Fadden)
Cover design by Helios Productions
Book design by Jerry Lee Hutchens
Illustrations by Kahionhes

Book Publishing Company
P.O. Box 99
Summertown, TN 38483
1-888-260-8458

02 01 00 99   4 3 2 1

ISBN 1-57067-082-X

Tehanetorens
    Wampum belts of the Iroquois / by Tehanetorens.
        p.   cm.
    Summary: Describes the nature and significance of Indian wampum belts, focusing on their history and uses by the Iroquois.
    ISBN 1-57067-082-X
    1. Wampum belts Juvenile literature. 2. Iroquois Indians--Social life and customs Juvenile literature.   [1. Wampum belts.
    2. Iroquois Indians--Social life and customs.   3. Indians of North America--Social life and customs.] I. Title.
    E99.I7T48   1999
    974.7'0049755--dc21   99-33789
                                                            CIP

Dedication

I, Tehanetorens, dedicate this book on wampum belts to my good friend and Shawnee Sister, White Water (Viola Farver) of Harrisburg, Pennsylvania, whose interest in the welfare of all Indian People, whose hospitality and friendship for any hungry or exhausted Indian knocking on her door, whose love and consideration for our animal and bird friends and whose dedication toward those things of Mother Earth which are good, has been an inspiration to me.

Six Nations Indian Museum
Onchiota, New York 12989

Niehweh Kowa

Through the interest and generosity of the Board of Trustees of the America The Beautiful Fund of New York who donated the necessary funds for purchase of material— wampum beads, thread, needles, lumber, frames, transportation and encouragement—it was possible for the students of the Onkwehonwe Neha or The Indian Way School at Akwesasne Mohawk Nation to do this project of making of authentic, bead for bead, exact copies of the sacred Iroquois wampum belts and strings, with descriptions of their meanings and how each fits into the history of the Iroquois.

We appreciate the kindness of the New York State Council of the Arts and the National Endowment For The Arts for making this project possible. Your thoughtfulness, wisdom, and encouragement are appreciated by not only myself as a teacher, but by the young Mohawk students of the Alternate School at Akwesasne Mohawk Nation.

Tehanetorens

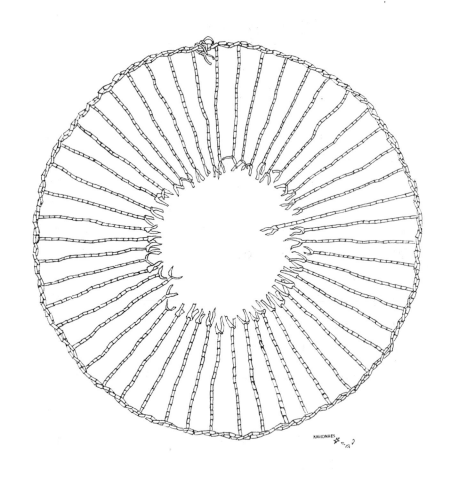

CIRCLE WAMPUM
Foundation of the Iroquois Confederacy

Wampum Belts
of the
Iroquois

*Pre-contact Mohawk chief with
wampum earrings, armband, and necklace.*

Wampum Belts
by Tehanetorens

To most people a wampum belt means any beaded belt made by Indians. Glass beads were introduced by white traders, and with these the Indian people did beautiful embroidery work. Before the introduction of glass beads, embroidery work was made with porcupine quills. The long hair from the bell or chin whiskers of moose was also used. With the introduction of the crude glass bead, the far more artistic porcupine quill and moose hair embroidery became a lost skill.

The true wampum bead was not made of glass. Along the Atlantic coastal waters from Cape Cod to Florida is found the quahog or round clam shell. Using this material the coastal Indian peoples made wampum beads. These were long, cylinder-shaped beads about one-fourth inch long and one-eighth of an inch in diameter in both white and purple. In ancient times wampum was strung on thread made of twisted elm bark. The word wampum is an Algonquin Indian term for these shell beads used by the Indians of the New England states. In the Seneca language it is called Ote-ko-a, a word that is the name of a small fresh water spiral shell. "Wampum" is the name that has survived to the present day. The early Indians of the Atlantic seaboard used this white and purple wampum for personal decorations as well as for trading purposes. Belts, wrist bands, earrings, necklaces, and headbands of wampum were observed by early white colonists while visiting New England Indians. The Indian people originally drilled this wampum shell with stone or reed drills. Later, iron drills were substituted.

Long Island Indians were especially skilled at manufacturing wampum. The process was simple, but it took long hours of practice before one was good at it. It took a great deal of patience and labor to make these beads. First the shell had to be broken into white or purple cubes. These cubes were clamped into a fissure split of a narrow stick. This was placed into a larger sapling splint in the same way. They were put on a firm support and a weight adjusted to cause the split to grip the shell firmly, holding it securely. A drill was braced against a solid object on the worker's chest and adjusted to the center of the cubes. A pump or bow drill rotated the drill. From a container placed over the closely clamped shell cube drops of water fell on the drill to keep it cool. One had to be careful that the shell did not break because of over heating caused by friction. According to Iroquois tradition, peach pits were broken and boiled in water. The resulting liquid made the shell soft during the drilling process. When a hole was drilled half way through the shell, it was reversed and a hole was drilled from the other side. The next part of the process was to shape and smooth the outside of the wampum bead. The beads were strung on lengths of thread or string and worked back and forth in a grooved stone. Five- to ten-foot lengths of wampum could be made in one day.

Even European settlers became wampum makers, and the first money of the American colonists was wampum. Wampum has often been called the money of Indians, but this is not true. Indians did not use it as currency in any way. By 1627 the Dutch were busy making counterfeit wampum. As late as the year 1875, a German community in Bergen, New Jersey, was busy making wampum for trade with the Indians.

At first only the coastal Indians had wampum. The east end of Long Island was the original seat of wampum trade. The Narragansett Indians who were related to these Long Island people soon controlled the wampum trade. They supplied the nations of the interior with their wampum, which was exchanged for furs from the western Indians.

Our Iroquois People used wampum for official purposes as well as for religious ceremonies. According to tradition, wampum was introduced to the Iroquois by Hiawatha (Ayonwatha) at the time of the founding of the League of the Five Nations. Hiawatha decreed and regulated its use. He taught the Five Nations that wampum should bring peace and bind peace and take the place of blood. He first introduced it to the Mohawks, and after telling the Council of its use, his co-worker, Deganawidah, used wampum to console or wipe away the tears of Hiawatha, whose heart was heavy because of the loss of his daughters. This was the first Condolence Ceremony and it has existed without change down to the present day. The first wampum used by Hiawatha was made from fresh water shells. There are traditions among the Iroquois that before shell wampum was known to the Five Nations wampum was made from wood stained black and white. An Onondaga tradition says that porcupine quills were first used as wampum. A Mohawk tradition says that the first wampum was made from the quills of the eagle. At any rate, Hiawatha seems to have been the first to use shell wampum for ceremonial purposes.

As wampum became more plentiful, it was used more and more until it came to be regarded as something sacred. Wampum strings served as credentials or as a certificate of authority. No Iroquois chief would listen to a messenger or pay attention to a report until he received official information through a runner who carried the proper wampum string or belt. Wampum guaranteed a message or a promise. Treaties meant nothing unless they were accompanied by wampum. Belts were given and received at treaties as seals of friendship.

No Iroquois individual or nation would think of breaking a word or treaty if the treaty was made over a sacred wampum belt. With every important treaty, wampum belts were exchanged. Sometimes as many as forty belts were exchanged at a single council. Likewise, every law passed by the Iroquois Council was recorded with a certain string or belt of wampum. The treaty or law that went with the wampum was memorized by certain trained individuals.

The Onondaga Nation, whose country was situated in the center of Iroquois Land, was chosen not only to be the Keepers of the Sacred Fire (Capitol) of the Iroquois Confederacy, but as the Keepers of the Wampum or records, as well.

Twice a year at a special council, a Wampum Keeper would gather the people and, taking each wampum belt and or string, would hold it aloft so that all could see. He would then recite the message or law that went with the particular wampum that he held. After reciting its meaning, the belt or string was passed from hand to hand among the entire gathering so that its design and meaning would always be remembered. At that time younger warriors who had been selected because of their keen minds were given special training and instruction by the older wampum keepers. These young men would some day become Keepers of the Wampum, and it was necessary that their training started early. It has been recorded by early white men that a wampum keeper, several years after the treaty had been made, could hold the belt that went with the treaty and repeat the entire message word for word without error, even though some of the treaties and promises were quite lengthy.

It is said that before wampum was introduced the wing of an eagle was given to sanction a treaty. In historical times beaver skins and painted sticks were used to replace wampum when it was scarce.

Six strings of purple wampum united at one end stand for the Six Nations. When this was laid in a circle, the council was open. When it was taken up, it meant that the council was over. Each nation of the Iroquois has a special string of wampum that represents their people. These are as follows:

Mohawks—six strings tied together, two purple beads to one white.

Oneidas—seven strings tied together, almost all purple beads.

Onondagas—four strings tied together, two purple beads to one white.

Senecas—four strings tied together, two purple beads alternated with two white.

Cayugas—six strings tied together, all purple beads.

When a speaker at an Iroquois council addressed a particular nation, he picked up and held in his hands that particular nation's wampum strings.

Notes

While reading a wampum belt, special care was made to hold the belt correctly. Usually when the message or speech was half finished, the speaker would turn the belt over.

A certain amount of wampum could ransom a murderer or captured prisoner.

A clan, one of whose members had been killed, could hand a wampum belt to a noted warrior. If the belt was accepted by the warrior, it meant that he would take over the responsibility of getting revenge for the clan and thus uphold their honor, the honor of the members. If the warrior let the belt fall, it mean that he would not accept the responsibility.

White wampum was the emblem of something good, of peace and purity. Purple wampum meant more important affairs of a civic nature.

A belt painted red was a war belt. If such a belt was sent to a nation, it was an invitation for them to join in the war. If the belt was taken, it meant that the nation would accept the invitation. If at the council it was thrown to the ground, it meant that the nation would not join in the war.

Wampum is still used in the ceremony of raising up a new Chief and in the Iroquois Thanksgivings and Kariwiio Ceremonies.

Every Chief of the Confederacy and every Clan Mother has a certain string or strings of wampum that is their certificate of office.

Invitation wampum for a civil or religious council is still used. A small stick attached to the wampum strings and covered

*First Grand Council with Peacemaker
holding white wampum belt.*

with notches tells the number of days before the council is to be held.

When a Head Chief or lesser chief of the Confederacy dies, a runner is sent to each nation carrying proper wampum strings. He walks from one end of the reservation to the other, and every once in awhile he will give a certain call (Kwee!). If he gives the call three times, one call after another, it tells the people that a head Chief has died. If he gives the call once at certain intervals, it means that a War Chief has died. His walk ends at the Council House, and there he tells the chiefs the sad news, showing proper wampum strings.

Because of the scarcity of wampum, only wampum strings are used today. Most of the old belts are lost. Many, through one way or another, have found their way to the show cases of museums. A few individual Indians have hidden away some of the old wampum belts.

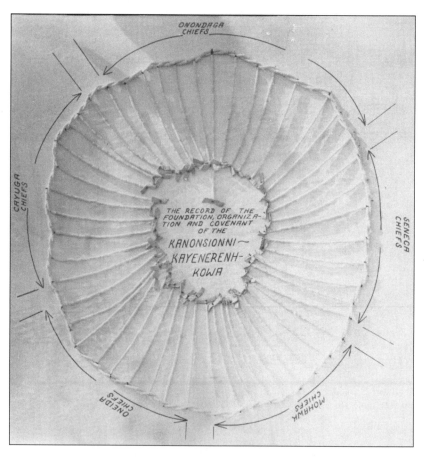

ONONDAGA CHIEFS

CAYUGA CHIEFS

SENECA CHIEFS

THE RECORD OF THE FOUNDATION, ORGANIZATION AND COVENANT OF THE

KANONSIONNI —

KAYENERENH-KOWA

ONEIDA CHIEFS

MOHAWK CHIEFS

The Charter of the League of The Five Nations

This is a record of the foundation of the Confederacy when it was formed around 1452 (or much earlier) by the Great Peacemaker and his helper Ayonwatha (Hiawatha). Of all Iroquois wampum records, this is the most sacred. Each of the fifty strings represents one of the chiefs of the original Five Nations, the Mohawks, Oneidas, Onondagas, Cayugas and Senecas. When the Confederacy was formed, the Peacemaker had each of the fifty chiefs join hands in a circle, and he ordained that all should be of equal rank and carry individual titles. So that they should never forget their titles and their positions in the Council House, this wampum record was made.

The First Chief of the Wolf Clan of the Mohawks, Sarenhowane, was appointed to keep this sacred wampum. During the Revolutionary War, the keeper of this particular wampum circle was a noted Mohawk warrior called Dewaserageh (Two Axe). For safe keeping, Two Axe placed this wampum, along with others, in a brass kettle and buried it under a bush beside Osagundaga Creek which runs into the Mohawk River. For eight years it was thus hidden. When the Revolutionary War was over, Mohawks returned and dug it up, carrying it with them to Grand River Lands where it was used to renew the Council Fire of the Six Nations. When the ceremony was over, it was again given to the hereditary keeper.

The large circle formed by two entwined strings means, respectively, The Great Peace and The Great Law (Kaianerekowa) that was established by the Five Nations. The fifty wampum strings represent the fifty Chiefs of the Confederacy. The longer wampum strings stand for the seventh Onondaga Chief who bears the title of Hononwiyendeh, who was appointed Keeper of all of the other records of the League. It serves as a guide when the record is read and shows the arrangements of the Chiefs in their proper order. White wampum means purity and peace which also means that Chiefs must never go to war. This sacred wampum is placed as in the above order with all of the fifty strings turned in toward the center. There are fourteen Chiefs representing the Onondagas, eight representing the Senecas, nine for the Mohawks, nine for the Oneidas, and ten for the Cayugas, who were thus to the right of the Onondagas. It was in this same order that the Chiefs took their seats in the Council House.

The Mohawks, if they were introducing a question, referred it first to the Chiefs of the Senecas who sat on their right. When the Senecas decided, the Mohawks referred it to the chiefs of the Oneidas and Cayugas. After their decision, the Mohawks laid it before the Onondaga Chiefs, who could express an independent opinion only if the other nations had disagreed.

It is provided thus: There are now the Five Nations League Chiefs standing with joined hands in a circle. This signified and provided that should any one of the chiefs of the League leave the council and the League, his crown of deer antlers, the emblems of his chieftainship title, together with his birthright, would lodge on the arms of the Union Chiefs whose hands were so joined. He forfeited his title, and the crown fell from his brow, but it remained in the League. A further meaning of this is that if at any time one of the chiefs chose to submit to the law of a foreign people, he was no longer in but out of the League, and persons of this class shall be called "They have alienated themselves," (Tehonatonkoton). Likewise, such persons who submitted to laws of foreign nations forfeited all birthrights and claims on the League of the Five Nations and territory. You, The League of Five Nations Chiefs, be firm so that if a tree shall fall upon your joined hands, it shall not separate you or weaken your hold. So shall the strength of your union be preserved.

"It Is Provided Thus:"

Wampum belts are formal records of momentous events. This book includes belts established as part of the Great Law, wampum belts which serve as official record of subsequent Iroquois Confederacy religious, political, and social history, and additional commentary. The phrase "It is provided thus:" as used by Tehanetorens denotes the instructions and symbols formulated by the Peacemaker and Hiawatha (Ayonwatha) and provided to the the people by the Peacemaker at the establishment of the Confederacy.

Hiawatha (Ayonwatha) Belt

The Hiawatha (Ayonwatha) Belt is a broad dark belt of wampum of thirty-eight rows, having a white heart or Great Tree in the center, on either side of which are two white squares, all connected with the heart by white rows of wampum shall be the emblem of the unity of

Hiawatha (Ayonwatha) Belt held by Mike Jock.

the Five Nations. The first of the squares on the left represents the Mohawk Nation and its territory. The second square on the left and the one near the heart, represents the Oneida Nation and its territory. The white heart or tree in the middle represents the Onondaga nation and its territory, and it also means that the heart of the Five Nations is single in its loyalty to The Great Peace—that the Great Peace is lodged in the heart—(meaning with Onondaga confederate Chiefs), and that the Council Fire is to burn there at Onondaga for the Five Nations. Further, it means that the authority is given to advance the cause of peace whereby hostile nations out of the Confederacy shall cease warfare. The white square to the right of the heart represents the Cayuga Nation and its territory, and the fourth and last square represents the Seneca Nation and its territory. The two lines extending out from each side of the squares of the belt, from the Mohawk and Seneca Nations, represents the Path of Peace by which other nations are welcomed to travel, to come and take shelter beneath the Great Tree of Peace or join the Iroquois Confederacy. White here shall symbolize that no evil or jealous thoughts shall creep into the minds of the leaders, the Chiefs, while in council under the Great Peace. White, in this case, is the emblem of peace, love, charity, and equity, and it surrounds and guards the Five Nations.

Wing or Dust Fan of The Confederate Nations

This belt is the widest belt known. It represents an ever-growing tree. It is provided thus:

I am Dekanawidah and with the Five Nations Confederate Chiefs I plant the Tree of The Great Place. I plant it in your territory, Adadarho, and the Onondaga Nation, in the territory of you who are The Firekeepers.

— I name the Tree, The Tree Of The Great Long Leaves. Under the shade of this Tree Of The Great Peace, we spread the soft, white feathery down of the globe thistle as seats for you, Adadarho, and your cousin Chiefs.

— We place you upon these seats, spread soft with the feathery down of the globe thistle, there beneath the shade of the spreading branches of the Tree Of Peace. There shall you sit and watch the Council Fire of the Confederacy of the Five Nations, and all of the affairs of the Five Nations shall be transacted at this place before you, Adadarho, and your cousin chiefs, by The Confederate Chiefs of The Five Nations.

— If any man or any nation outside of the Five Nations shall obey the Laws of The Great Peace and make known their disposition to the Chiefs of the Confederacy, they may trace the Roots to the Tree, and if their minds are clean and they are obedient and promise to obey the wishes of the Confederate Council, they shall be welcome to take shelter beneath The Tree Of The Long Leaves.

— We place at the top of The Tree Of The Long Leaves an Eagle who is able to see afar. If he sees in the distance any evil approaching or any danger threatening, he will at once warn the People of The Confederacy.

— To you, Adadarho, and the Onondaga cousin Chiefs, all of the Confederate Chiefs have entrusted the caretaking and the watching of the Five Nations Council Fire.

This belt represents an everlasting tree. It grows high and its top reaches the Spirit World that all nations may see it. Under this Tree the Peacemaker placed a general fire to burn forever, Onondaga, the Council Place of the Five Nations. At that council it was said, "This is

Harold Edwards, Jr. holding Everlasting Tree Belt.

the last belt which we make confirming the laws which we have adopted." At this council the Peacemaker said, "As long as you follow the laws of The Five Nations, you will be in prosperity and happiness, but whenever our people do not heed the instructions we give, then there will come a state of dissension among our people." He, the Great Law Giver, The Peacemaker, also said, "When you are in a state of great confusion, I will return and again plant The Tree Of Peace, and it will become stronger than before, that in the end, the government and laws of the Confederacy will influence the entire world."

This ever-growing Tree Belt symbolizes the permanence of The Iroquois Confederacy. It was displayed in confederate councils and was therefore sometimes called "The Wing of The Chief Royaneh." It was to protect the Council and to keep the eyes of the 50 civil leaders free from dust or harmful thoughts. It was displayed when ever the League Constitution was recited.

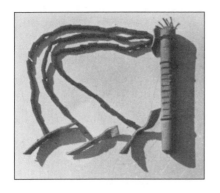

Invitation Wampum Strings

Upper left: purple wampum used to call a condolence council for a principal chief.

Center: purple wampum used in calling a mourning council or condolence for raising a secondary chief or war chief.

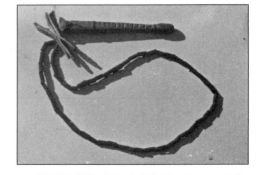

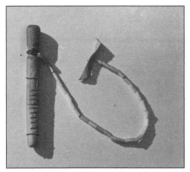

Lower left: white wampum used to call a religious council.

The number of notches on the sticks tell the number of days before the council.

- Okkwehonweneha or Indian Way School -

Wampum Strings

It is provided thus: Any Chief of the League of the Five Nations may construct shell strings or wampum belts of any size or length as pledges or records of matters of national or international importance. When it is necessary to dispatch a shell string by a war chief or other messenger as a token of a summons, the messenger shall recite the contents of the string to the party to whom it is sent. That party will repeat the message and return the shell string, and if there has been a summons, he shall make ready for his journey. Any of the people of the Five Nations may use shells or wampum as the record of a pledge, contract, or an agreement entered into, and the same shall be binding as soon as the shell strings shall have been exchanged by both parties.

It is provided thus: When a Chief of the League dies, the surviving relatives shall immediately dispatch a messenger, a member of another clan, to the chiefs in another locality. When the runner comes within hailing distance of the locality, he shall utter a sad wail thusly, "Kwa-ah! Kwa!" The sound shall be repeated three times and then again and again at intervals as many times as the distance shall require. When the runner arrives at the settlement, the people shall assemble at the Council House, and one must ask him the nature of his sad message. He shall then say, "Let us consider (Rakwennikooriak)." Then he shall tell them of the death of the Chief. He shall deliver to them a string of shells or wampum and say, "Here is the testimony. You have heard the message." He may return home. It now becomes the duty of the Chiefs of the locality to send runners to other localities, and each locality shall send messengers until all Chiefs are notified. Runners shall travel night and day.

It is provided thus: When the Chiefs of the League take occasion to dispatch a messenger in behalf of the Council of the League, they shall wrap up any matter they may send, and instruct the messenger to remember his errand, to turn not aside but to proceed faithfully to his destination and deliver his message according to every instruction.

It is provided thus: If a message born by a runner is the warning of an invasion, he shall whoop, "Kwa-ah! Kwa-ah!" twice and repeat at short intervals, then again at a longer interval. If a human is found dead, the finder shall not touch the body, but return home immediately, shouting at short intervals, "Koo-weh!"

Peace Pact Wampum Strings

It is provided thus: A bunch of wampum strings, three spans of the hand in length, the upper half of the bunch being white and the lower half black, and formed from equal contributions of the men of the Five Nations, shall be the token that the men have combined themselves into one head, one body, and one thought. It shall symbolize their ratification of the Peace Pact of the league, whereby the Chiefs of the Five Nations have established The Great Peace. The white portion of the shell strings represents the women, and the black portion the men. The black portion, furthermore, is a token of power and authority vested in the Men of The Five Nations—this bunch of wampum vests the people with the right to correct their erring chiefs. In case a part of the chiefs or all of them pursue a course not vouched for by the people and heed not the third warning of their women relatives (Wasenesawenrate), then the matter shall be taken to the general council of the women of the Five Nations. If the chiefs notified and warned three times fail to heed, then the case falls into the hands of the men of the Five Nations. The War Chiefs shall then, by right of such power and authority, enter the open council to warn the chief or chiefs to return from their wrong doings. If the chiefs heed the warning, they shall say, "We shall reply tomorrow." If then an answer is returned in favor of justice and in accord with the Great Law, then the chiefs shall immediately pledge themselves again, by again furnishing the necessary shells for the pledge. Then shall the War Chief or Chiefs exhort the chiefs, urging them to be just and true.

— Shall it happen that the chiefs refuse to heed the third warning, then two courses are open: either the men may decide in their council to depose the chief or chiefs, or to club them to death with war clubs. Should they in their council decide to take the first course, the War Chief shall address the chief or chiefs, saying, "Since you, the Chiefs of the Five Nations, have refused to return to the procedure of the Constitution, we now declare your seats vacant, and we take off your horns, the token of your chieftainship, and others shall be chosen and installed in your seats. Therefore vacate your seats!" Should

Frame with wampum strings of black and white presented by Lynn Montour.

the men in their council adopt the second course, the War Chief shall order his men to enter the council and take positions beside the errant chiefs sitting between them wherever possible. When this is accomplished, the War Chief, holding in his hand a bunch of black wampum strings, shall say to the erring chiefs, "So now, Chiefs of the Five Nations, harken to these last words from your men. You have not heeded the warning of the general council of women, and you have not heeded the warning of the men of the nation, all urging you to the right course of action. Since you are determined to resist and to withhold justice from your people, there is only one course for us to adopt." At this point, the War Chief shall drop the bunch of black wampum, and the men shall spring to their feet and club the erring chiefs to death. Any erring chief may become submissive before the War Chief lets fall the black wampum. Then his execution is withheld. The black wampum here used symbolizes that the power to execute is buried, but it may be raised up again by the men. It is buried but when the occasion arises, they may pull it up and derive their power and authority to act as here described.

Alvin Jock holding Women's Nominating Belt.

Women's Nominating Belt

Among the Iroquois, women have the privilege of nominating the Chiefs.

It is provided thus: We give and assign the sacred chieftainship titles and the soil of our land to all of our Mothers, the Women of the Five Nations, and they shall be proprietors of the same. If they see their Chiefs acting contrary to constitutional justice, that they are not counciling for the interest of the people generally, the women relatives of the erring chiefs shall come (the War Chief acting in their behalf) before that Council to warn them three times, and no more, to return to justice and council for the interest and welfare of the people generally. If he or they disregard their warning, even the third time, he or they then shall be dispossessed of their title. They, the women, will then make known the fact to the rest of the Chiefs of the Nation, whereof they are members who will then sanction their deed. Then the women will select another one of their Clan to fill the vacancy thus made and will notify the rest of the Chiefs, whereof they are members, of their choice and who will be their Chiefs in the future. In such case the Chiefs have only one course, that is, to sanction their deed.

It is provided thus: That the lineal descent of the Five Nations shall run in the female side and the women shall be considered as the progenitors of the nation, and the title of ownership of the land or

soil of the Nation's country shall be vested in the said women. The descendants of the women shall follow the statues of their Mothers with respect to clans which they are the distinguishing marks of families.

It is provided thus: That the women of every clan of the Five Nations shall have a Council Fire (voice) which shall ever be burning for the purpose of holding a council of the Women of the clan when in their opinion it is necessary and advantageous to the people and their commonwealth. The decision, conclusion, or recommendation of such a council shall be introduced for consideration into the Council of the Confederate Chiefs by the War Chief of that clan.

Clan mother with a war chief who holds the Women's Nominating Belt as two colonials watch.

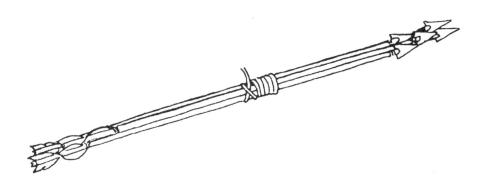

Record of Chiefs of Mohawk Nation

Mohawk Clan Chieftanship wampum strings are a record of the leaders of the Mohawk Nation. The keeper of this record was of the Wolf Clan, whose title is Sarehowane. There should be similar records of the other four nations of the original Iroquois states.

The Mohawk Nations has nine chiefs, thus the nine strings in this record. The small string of wampum uniting them symbolizes that the chiefs shall all be of one mind. The nine wampum strings are in three groups representing the three clans of the Mohawk Nation: the Turtle clan, the Wolf Clan, and the Bear Clan. Each clan is represented at the Mohawk Council by three chiefs. The string standing for the first Chief of each clan is of white wampum only. Two purple wampum among the white represents the Second Chief, and the string representing the Third Chief has three purple wampum. The wampum strings lay with the all-white string on the left and read from left to right:

TURTLE CLAN
1st Chief: Tekarihoken (The Mediator)
2nd Chief: Ayonwatha (Hiawatha) (He Who Combs)
3rd Chief: Satekariwate (The Clear Thinker)

WOLF CLAN
1st Chief: Sarenhowane (Majestic Tree)
2nd Chief: Teyonhekwen (He Who Has Two Lives)
3rd Chief: Orenrekowa (Great Limb On A Tree)

BEAR CLAN
1st Chief: Tehanakarine (He Who Drags Horns)
2nd Chief: Ostawenserentha (He Hangs Up The Rattles)
3rd Chief: Soskoharowane (A Great Bush)

Pat Jock displaying panel with mounted
Mohawk Clan Chieftainship strings.

It is provided thus: The Council of the Mohawks shall be divided into three parties: Tekarihoken, Ayonwatha (Hiawatha), and Satekariwate are the first. Sarenhowane, Teyonhekwen, and Orenrekowa are the second. Tehanakarine, Ostawenserentha, and Siskoharowane are the third. The third party is to listen only to the discussion of the first and second parties. If an error is made, or the proceeding irregular, they are to call attention to it, and when the case is right and properly decided by the two parties, they shall confirm the decision of the two parties and refer the case to the Seneca statesmen for their decision. When the Seneca statesmen have decided, in accord with the Mohawk Statesman, the case or question shall be referred to the Cayuga and Oneida Statesmen on the opposite side of the house.

It is provided thus: In all cases of passing a law, the procedure must be as follows: When the Mohawk and Seneca Chiefs have agreed unanimously upon a question, they report their decision to the Cayuga and Oneida Chiefs who shall council upon the question and report a unanimous decision to the Mohawk Chiefs. The Mohawk Chiefs then report the decision on the case to the Firekeepers (Onondaga) who shall render a decision as they see fit in case of a disagreement by the two bodies, or confirm the decision to the Mohawk Chiefs who announce it to the open council.

It is provided thus: If through any misunderstanding or disagreement on the part of the Firekeepers that they decide different with that of the two sides, the two sides shall then reconsider or council the matter again, and if their decisions are still the same as before, they shall report it again to the Firekeepers who then must confirm their joint decision.

War Belt

It is provided thus: There shall be one War Chief from each nation, and their duties shall be to carry messages for their Chiefs, and to take up arms in case of emergency. They shall not participate in the proceedings of the Council of the League, but shall watch its progress and in case of an erroneous action by a Chief, they shall receive the complaints of the people and convey the warning of the women to him. The people who wish to convey messages to the Chiefs of the League shall do so through the War Chief of their nation. It shall always be his duty to lay the cases, questions, and propositions of the people before the Council of the League.

It is provided thus: When a War Chief dies, another shall be installed by the same rites as that by which a Chief is installed.

It is provided thus: If a War Chief acts contrary to instructions or against the provisions of the Laws of the Great Peace, doing so in the capacity of his office, he shall be deposed by his women relatives and by his men relatives. Either the women or the men alone or jointly may act in such a case. The women title holders shall then choose another candidate.

It is provided thus: When the proposition to establish The Great Peace is made to a foreign nation, it shall be done in mutual council. The foreign nation is to be persuaded by reason and urged to come into the Great Peace. If the Five Nations fail to obtain the consent of the nation at the first council, a second council shall be held, and upon a second failure, a third council shall be held, and this third council shall end the peaceful methods of persuasion. At the third council, the War chief of the Five Nations shall address the chief of the foreign nation and request him three times to accept The Great Peace. If refusal steadfastly follows, the War Chief shall let the bunch of white wampum drop from his outstretched hand to the ground, and shall bound quickly forward and club the offending chief to death. War shall thereby be declared, and the War Chief shall have his warriors to back any emergency. War must continue until the contest is won by the Five Nations.

Harold Edwards, Jr. holding War Belt.

It is provided thus: When the Chiefs of the Five Nations propose to meet in conference with a foreign nation with proposals for an acceptance of The Great Peace, a large band of warriors shall conceal themselves in a secure place from the espionage of the foreign nation but as near at hand as possible. Two warriors shall accompany the Union Chief who carries the proposals, and these warriors shall be especially cunning. Should the chief be attacked, these warriors shall hasten back to the army of warriors with the news of the calamity which fell through the treachery of the foreign nation.

It is provided thus: When the Five Nations Council declares war, any Chief of the League may enlist with the warriors by temporarily renouncing his sacred chieftainship title which he holds through the nomination of his women relatives. The title then reverts to them and they may bestow it upon another temporarily until the war is over, when the Chief, if living, may resume his title and sat in the council.

Red Painted War Belt

Any belt could be used as a war belt by painting it red. It is provided thus: The title names of the War Chiefs of the League shall be as follows:

Ayonewehs, War Chief under Chief Takarihoken

(Mohawk)

Kahonwaitiron, War Chief under Chief Otatsheteh

(Oneida)

Ayentes, War Chief under Chief Atotarho

(Onondaga)

Wenens, War Chief under Chief Dekaenyon

(Cayuga)

Shoneratowaneh, War Chief under Chief Skanyatariio

(Seneca)

It is provided thus: The women heirs of each head chief's title shall be the heirs of the War Chief's title of their respective chief. It is provided thus; The War Chiefs shall be selected from the eligible sons of the female families holding the head chieftainship title. It is provided thus: When the men of the League, now called forth to become warriors, are ready for battle with an obstinate opposing nation that has refused to accept the Great Peace, then one of the five War Chiefs shall be chosen by the warriors of the League to lead the army into battle. It shall be the duty of the War Chief so chosen to come before his warriors and address them. His aim shall be to impress upon them the necessity of good behavior and strict obedience to the commands of the War Chiefs. He shall deliver an oration exhorting them with great zeal to be brave and courageous and never to be guilty of cowardice. At the conclusion of his oration he shall march forward and commence a War Song, and he shall sing,

> Now I am greatly surprised
> And therefore I shall use it,
> The power of my War Song.
> I am of the Five Nations,

And I shall make an appeal
To the mighty Creator.
He has furnished this army.
My warriors shall be mighty
In the strength of the Master of Life.
Between him and my song they are,
For it was he who gave the song,
This War Song that I sing.

It is provided thus: When the warriors of the Five Nations are on an expedition against the enemy, the War Chief shall sing the War Song as he approaches the country of the enemy and not cease until his scouts have reported that the army is near the enemy's lines, wherein the War Chief shall approach with great caution and prepare for the attack.

It is provided thus: When peace shall have been established by the termination of the war against a foreign nation, the War Chief shall cause all the weapons of war to be taken from the nation. Then the Great Peace shall be established and that nation shall observe all the rules of the Great Peace for all time to come.

It is provided thus: Whenever a foreign nation is conquered or has by their own will accepted the Great Peace, their own system of internal government may continue, but they must cease all warfare against other nations. This certain wampum belt of black background beads shall be the emblem of the authority of the Five War Chiefs to take up the weapons of war and with their men to resist invasions. This shall be called a war in defense of the territory.

Belt of four sets of joined diamonds with four white paths on one end held by Tina Big Bear Anderson.

Donehogawah War Belt

This belt was formerly held by Donehogawah or General Ely S. Parker. It means "Five Council Fires" or "Death Belt" of the five Iroquois Nations, the Confederacy of the Iroquois. The Death Belts were in the custody of The Keepers of the East and West Door of the Ho-de-ne-sau-neh. This one was always held by the Do-ne-ho-ga-wah, the Keeper of The Western Door, the Seneca nation, who was the guardian of the Western Door, the watcher and army guard of the Confederacy. (The Mohawks of The Eastern Door likewise had their copy of this particular belt.) This belt signified death or war against some other nation or nations. When it was sent to the East Door, the Mohawk Council, it was held and passed on to the Councils of War of each of the nations, Seneca, Cayuga, Onondaga, Oneida, Mohawk, until returned by the Mohawks, which signalled was that the war must begin at once. It represented death or extermination, or adoption by the Iroquois after conquest, whichever was decided on. It was painted with red paint on its journey through the nations. The Tonawanda Senecas were the last to hold this particular belt. At the Condolence Council of General Parker, another Donehogawah Chief was raised as the successor of General Parker.

The five open hexagons represent the Five Nations. The three white wampum lines at the ends of the belt represent the three warnings that were always given a hostile or enemy nation to cease warfare and obey the laws of The Great Peace. After the third warning had been ignored, the combined Iroquois attacked the enemy people but only after they had been given three chances to change their minds or hearts. If a War Belt was returned by a nation with a string of white wampum, it meant that the nation who had sent the belt back did not want to take part.

A nation could carry on a war of its own if it wished, but this did not happen often. A general war could be determined only by the Grand Council at Onondaga, and all must consent to such a war. It had to be unanimous.

Dan Thompson holding Donehogawah War Belt.

It is provided thus: Skanawati shall be vested with a double office duty and with double authority. One half of his being shall hold the statesman title, and the other half shall hold the title of War Chief. In the event of war, he shall notify the five War Chiefs of the League and he will command them to prepare for war, to have

their men ready at the appointed time and place for engagement with the enemy of the Great Peace.

It is provided thus: When the Council of the League has for its objective the establishment of The Great Peace among the people of an outside nation and that nation refuses to accept the Great Peace, then by such refusal they bring a declaration of war upon themselves from the Five Nations. Then shall the Five Nations seek to establish the Great Peace by conquest of the rebellious nation.

Wendy Montour holding Unity of The Clans Belt.

Belt of The
Unity of The Clans

This belt was one of the Constitutional Memorials and signified the essential unity of the clans "who sat opposite each other about the Fire." The white background signifies peace, unity, and friendship.

It is provided thus: That in the Confederate Iroquois Nation, the people bearing the same name, the same clan, shall recognize one another as relatives irrespective of their nation and shall treat one another as such. Therefore a man and woman of the same clan are forbidden to marry.

It is provided thus: When an infant of the Five Nations is given an authorized name at the Midwinter Festival or at the Green Corn, Strawberry, or Harvest Festival, one in the Cousinhood of which the infant is a member shall be appointed a speaker. He shall then announce to the opposite Cousinhood the names of the father and mother of the child, together with the clan of the mother. Then the speaker shall announce the child's name twice. The uncle of the child shall then take the child in his arms and walking up and down the room shall sing, "My head is firm! I am of the League." As he sings, the opposite cousinhood shall respond by chanting "Hyen, Hyen, Hyen, Hyen" until the song is ended.

It is provided thus: When a chieftainhood title becomes vacant through death or other causes, the Otiianer Women of the clan in which the title is hereditary shall hold a council and shall chose one of their sons to fill the office made vacant. Such a candidate shall not be the father of any chief of the League. If the choice is unanimous, the name is referred to the men relatives of the clan. If they shall disapprove, it shall be their duty to select a candidate from among their own number. If then the men and women are unable to decide which of the two candidates shall be named, then the matter shall be referred to the Chiefs of the League in the clan. They shall decide which candidate shall be named. If the men and women agree to a candidate, then his name shall be referred to the sister clans for confirmation. If the sister clans confirm the choice, they shall refer their action to the Chiefs of the League who shall ratify the choice and present it to their Cousin Chiefs, and if the Cousin Chiefs confirm the name, then the candidate shall be installed by the proper ceremony for the conferring of chieftainship titles.

Three Sisterhood

Long ago when the Mohawk People lived in villages beside the Mohawk River in what is now New York State, the Mohawk Clans lived in separate villages: Bear Clan People lived in one village, Turtle Clan People in another, and Wolf Clan People had their own village. There is a traditional story which tells of a Wolf Clan Village where there lived three Mohawk girls. These girls could never meet without quarreling with each other. They quarreled so often that other people began to notice them. Finally, because of this constant friction, an old woman who was wise and who was greatly respected by her people decided to do something about it. This pious woman's name was Konwahtjonhontyon (Forsaken Fireside). One by one she approached each girl individually and said to each of them, "I want you to visit my home at a certain time because I have something to say to you. I also have something to show you." When each girl showed up at the old woman's house they were surprised to meet the other two girls there also. Before they had time to start quarreling with each other, Konwahtjonhontyon said to them, "I am pleased that you have come and I have something to show you." She took them to her garden and pointed to a hill of corn, showing them how corn, beans, and squash plants were growing together in the same mound. She then said, "Look daughters, Our Creator gave us these foods. Our ancient Fathers learned that if these three plants are planted together in one hill, they will grow and thrive without hurting one another, yet each will maintain its own character. They—corn, bean, and squash—are three sisters and they grow together in harmony. You three sisters should note this. You must live together in the same way. I now want you to go home and I want you to think about what you have seen and what I have told you. In three days I want you to come back to my house. In three days I will explain the meaning of a wampum string that I am making."

In three days the girls retuned to the house of Konwahtjonhontyon. She then showed them the wampum strings that she had completed. She said, "The five dark strings in this wampum stand for the

A copy of Konwahtjonhontyon's Three Sisterhood Wampum
Strings mounted on a panel held by Edgar Jock.

Five Nations of the Iroquois Confederacy. Three of the six white strings at the end of this wampum represent you three girls. Now if any of you three sisters quarrel or break the rules that I am laying down for your behavior, I will replace a white bead with a dark bead in the white string that hangs beside the string that stands for you. Then you will be shamed before the whole village."

When Konwahtjonhontyon finished speaking, the three girls were silent. One by one they left and returned to their homes. Konwahtjonhontyon kept these wampum strings in her possession. Since that time other groups of three formed similar sisterhoods. These sisterhoods spread throughout the Five Nations Confederacy. At some ceremonial festival or council, three girls who had decided to form such a sisterhood would stand before the people. They would join hands before Konwahtjonhontyon and hear her explain the rules of the sisterhood; that each girl must live in peace, love, and good will with her two special sisters, that she must help them at all times, and must do the same with other sisterhood groups of three. Each girl then pledged her vow before all of the people.

These voluntary groups of three, all separate, yet all bound by the same rules, had a good influence on the young people of the Iroquois. Throughout its history there was never an occasion when the rules were broken in a sisterhood. This wampum record remains the same as it was when it was first put together by the wise old Mohawk lady who lived in the old Mohawk Country long ago with no dark beads mixed with the white.

Hospitality or Welcome Belt

This belt records certain laws of the Confederacy and was used in the League councils by the presiding Chief in welcoming other nation delegates. A review of some of these laws is as follows: It is provided thus, When a chieftainship title is to be conferred, the candidate chief shall furnish the cooked venison, the corn bread, and the the corn soup, together (with) other necessary things and the labor for the conferring of the title's festival. The Otiianer Women of the League, heirs of the chieftainship titles, shall elect two women of their family as cooks for the Chiefs when the people shall assemble at his house for business or other purposes. It is not good nor honorable for a Chief of the League to all his people whom he has called to go hungry. When a chief holds a conference in his home, his wife, if she wishes, may prepare the food for the Union Chiefs who assemble with him. This is an honorable right which she may exercise, and is an expression of her esteem.

Young Paul Boots holding Hospitality Belt.

Adodarhoh Belt

It is provided thus: To you, Adodarhoh and your cousin chiefs, fourteen of you altogether, this shall be your duty. You shall keep The Confederate Council Fire (Government) clean all around. You shall allow no dust or dirt to be seen around the Council Fire. I therefore lay a seagull wing near you. Take this wing and sweep the dust and dirt away from the Council Fire. If you see any crawling creature approaching the Confederate Council Fire, I lay a stick by you with which you are to pitch the crawling creature from the Council Fire, and your cousin chiefs will act with you at all times. Dust, dirt, and crawling creatures signify a matter or proposition brought before the Council which would be injurious to The Confederate Nation. If you and your chiefs fail to reject it alone, you shall call the rest of the Confederate Chiefs to your aid.

Mark Jock holding Adodarhoh Belt

Tina Big Bear Anderson holding Ransom Belt.

Ransom Belt

This belt was used by the women of the nation to symbolize their authority for adopting a prisoner of war. The belt removed the cloud of the women's mourning and made a son of the captive. It could save a life if presented by a woman.

It is provided thus: Any member of the Five Nations, who through esteem or other feelings, wishes to adopt an individual, a family, or a number of families, may offer adoption to him or them, and if accepted, the matter shall be brought to the attention of the Chiefs for confirmation and the Chiefs must confirm the adoption.

It is provided thus: When the adoption of anyone shall have been confirmed by the Chiefs of the Nation, the Chiefs shall address the people of the Nation and say, "Now you of our nation, be informed that those adopted have ceased forever to bear their birth nation's name and have buried it in the depth of the earth. Henceforth, let no one of our nation ever mention the original name or nation of their birth. To do so will hasten the end of our peace."

Don Fadden holding Chief's Pledge Wampum.

Chief's Pledge Wampum

It is provided thus: When a candidate chief is to be installed, he shall furnish four strings of shell wampum one span length bound together at one end. Such will constitute the evidence of his pledge to the Chiefs of the League that he will live according to the Constitution of the Great Peace and exercise justice in all affairs. When the pledge is finished, the speaker of the council must hold the wampum strings in his hand and address the opposite side of the council fire, and he shall begin his address saying:

"Now behold him. He has now become a chief of the League. See how splendid he looks." An address may then follow. At the end of it, he shall send the bunch of wampum strings to the opposite side— Elder or Younger Brothers, whichever it may be—and they shall be received as evidence of the pledge. Then the speaker of the opposite side says:

"We now do crown you with the sacred emblem of the Deer's antlers, the emblem of your chieftainship. You shall now become a mentor of the people of the Five Nations. The thickness of your skin shall be seven spans, which is to say that you shall be proof against anger, offensive actions, and criticism. Your heart shall be filled with peace and good will. Your mind shall be filled with a yearning for the welfare of the people of the League. With endless patience you shall carry out your duty, and your firmness shall be tempered with tenderness for your people. Neither anger nor fury shall find lodging in your mind. All your words and actions shall be marked with calm deliberation. In all your deliberations in the Council of the League, in your efforts at lawmaking, in all your official acts, self-interest shall be cast away. Do not cast over your shoulder behind you the warning of your Nephews and Nieces (your people) should they chide you for any error or wrong you may do, but return to the way of The Great Law which is right and just. Look and listen for the welfare of the whole people, and have always in view not only the present, but also the coming generations, even those whose faces are yet beneath the surface of the ground—the unborn of the future nation."

Condolence Strings

It is provided thus: If a chief of the League should die while the Council of the Five Nations is in session, the Council shall adjourn for ten days. No Council of the League shall sit within ten days of the death of a chief of the League.

If the Three Brothers (Ashennihontatakenah, the Mohawks, the Onondagas and the Senecas) should lose one of their chiefs by death, the Younger Brothers (Iatatekanah, the Cayugas, the Oneidas, and the Tuscaroras) shall come to the surviving chiefs of the Three Brothers on the tenth day and console them. If the Younger Brothers lose one of their chiefs, then the Three Elder Brothers shall come to them and console them. And the consolation shall be the reading of the contents of the thirteen strings of wampum used by Ayonwatha (Hiawatha). At the termination of this rite, a successor shall be appointed by the women heirs of the chieftainship title. If the women are not ready to place their nominee before the chiefs, the speaker shall say, "Come let us go out." All shall then leave the council or place of gathering. The speaker shall lead the way from the house by saying, "Let us depart to the edge of the woods and lie in wait on our bellies (Tenshakonatioswentarhese)."

Condolence Strings

Our Uncles, give us your ears, hear us. We have come to you to lament together, to console with you over your great loss, your bereavement. We now meet in great sorrow to mourn together over the death of our Brother Chief. We mourn your great loss. In our grief we will sit together and mingle our tears.

Wampum String One

We now take you by the hand and wipe the tears from off your eyes so that you may see clearly. This we say and do, we your brothers.

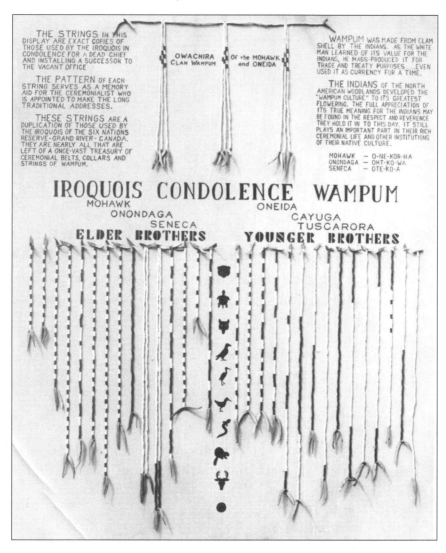

THE STRINGS IN THIS DISPLAY ARE EXACT COPIES OF THOSE USED BY THE IROQUOIS IN CONDOLENCE FOR A DEAD CHIEF AND INSTALLING A SUCCESSOR TO THE VACANT OFFICE

THE PATTERN OF EACH STRING SERVES AS A MEMORY AID FOR THE CEREMONIALIST WHO IS APPOINTED TO MAKE THE LONG TRADITIONAL ADDRESSES.

THESE STRINGS ARE A DUPLICATION OF THOSE USED BY THE IROQUOIS OF THE SIX NATIONS RESERVE-GRAND RIVER- CANADA. THEY ARE NEARLY ALL THAT ARE LEFT OF A ONCE-VAST TREASURY OF CEREMONIAL BELTS, COLLARS AND STRINGS OF WAMPUM.

OWACHIRA CLAN WAMPUM

Of the MOHAWK and ONEIDA

WAMPUM WAS MADE FROM CLAM SHELL BY THE INDIANS. AS THE WHITE MAN LEARNED OF ITS VALUE FOR THE INDIANS, HE MASS-PRODUCED IT FOR TRADE AND TREATY PURPOSES....EVEN USED IT AS CURRENCY FOR A TIME.

THE INDIANS OF THE NORTH AMERICAN WOODLANDS DEVELOPED THE "WAMPUM CULTURE" TO ITS GREATEST FLOWERING. THE FULL APPRECIATION OF ITS TRUE MEANING FOR THE INDIANS MAY BE FOUND IN THE RESPECT AND REVERENCE THEY HOLD IT IN TO THIS DAY. IT STILL PLAYS AN IMPORTANT PART IN THEIR RICH CEREMONIAL LIFE AND OTHER INSTITUTIONS OF THEIR NATIVE CULTURE.

MOHAWK ― O-NE-KOR-HA
ONONDAGA ― OHT-KO-WA
SENECA ― OTE-KO-A

IROQUOIS CONDOLENCE WAMPUM

MOHAWK
ONONDAGA
SENECA
ELDER BROTHERS

ONEIDA
CAYUGA
TUSCARORA
YOUNGER BROTHERS

"Iroquois Condolence Wampum" mounted on panel. Original panel is located on the left of the west wall of the first room of the Six Nations Indian Museum.

Wampum String Two

Now hear us again, this occurs when one of our number is removed by death. When a person is in great sorrow, his throat is stopped with grief and sadness. We now take you by the hand and remove the sorrow and obstruction out of your throat so that you may enjoy perfect breathing and speech.

Wampum String Three

Now hear us again, this occurs when one of your number is removed by death: it stops your ears. You cannot hear clearly. Such is your case now. So now we remove the grief from your ears. We unpluck and clean out your ears, so that you may hear distinctly when anyone addresses you.

Wampum String Four

Continue to hear the expression of us, your brothers. Ja-we-ka-ro-den is the liquid, the medicine, we now give you to drink. It will wash away the bitterness, the gall spots in your stomach. It will pervade your whole body and strengthen you. It will restore you to a perfect form of man. Your mind will become more easy. This we say and do, we your brothers.

Wampum String Five

Thus it occurs when one of your number is removed by death: your sight becomes dark. You cannot see clearly. You are blinded by grief. You lose sight of the sky and are crushed by sorrow. So now we brighten your eyes again. We remove the mist from your eyes that you may see the sun rising above the forest. This we say and do, we your brothers.

Wampum String Six

Thus it occurs when one of your number is removed by death: dark clouds cover the sky above you and there is no light around you. We place you where there is light so that you will see the people clearly and you will not lose the sight of heaven. We remove the dark clouds from above you that you will see your duties and perform for your people as usual. This we say and do, we your brothers.

Wampum String Seven

Thus it occurs when one of your number is removed by death: the sun is displaced in the sky. So now we restore the Sun in his place.

You will now see the Sun rising over the trees in the east. When Sun arrives in mid-sky, He will shine forth his rays around you and you will again see your duties. Your mind will again become easy and you will perform for your people. This we say and do, we your brothers.

Wampum String Eight

Continue to hear the expression of us, your brothers. Now when a person is brought to grief by death, such person's seat seems stained with human blood. Death has scattered dead bodies around you. The ashes of your fire are scattered. Therefore we now remove the dead bodies around you. We wipe off the blood stains with soft cloth so that your seat may be clean. The sticks of wood from your fire are scattered, caused by death. We your brothers, will gather up sticks of wood. We will rekindle the Council Fire. We now restore you to your seat so that your mind will now become easy and you will enjoy peace again. Now you again will labor freely for the people. This we say and do, we your brothers.

Wampum String Nine

Thus it occurs when one of your members is removed by death: one is in deep grief caused by the death of one of your Leaders. The head is bowed down in deep sorrow. As your heads are hanging down with sorrow, grief and sadness, we lift up your heads. We therefore cause you to stand upright again to resume your duties.

Wampum String Ten

Now my Uncle Chiefs, you have two relations, a Nephew and a Niece. They are watching your actions. They may see that you are doing wrong and taking a course that will cause your people, your children, to suffer ruin. Your Nephew or Niece (your people) will warn you if you go astray from your duty, the right course. They will tell you to return again and labor and legislate for the interest of the people. This we say and do, we your brothers.

Mohawk with wampum strings.

Wampum String Eleven

Now the remains of your chief is laid in the earth and a mound of clay covers the grave. We now level the grave and cover it up with nice grass and bushes. We place a good board over it so that the body may lie quietly in its resting place. When the scorching heat of the sun shines on the grave, the board will protect it and the heat will not go through to the body. The body will also be protected from the heavy rains so that it will not spoil. It will be preserved and protected. Nothing will disturb the body and it will rest in peace.

Wampum String Twelve

Continue to listen, our brothers. We have hung up a pouch on a slanting pole. We put a short string of wampum in the pouch. This is to be used by someone who has lost one of their number by death. It is to encourage and cheer up their downcast spirits.

Wampum String Thirteen

It is said that it is bad for one to allow his mind to be troubled too greatly with sorrow. Because of this one may be led to think of destroying himself. We now put two poles together. We place a torch or light upon this. We all have an equal share in this light. If you see anything that will tend to our destruction, you will take that light and go and warn the Confederate People without delay. You will call all of the Confederate Chiefs to their places, and they will each perform the duties conferred upon each of them. This we say and do, we your brothers.

Now we return to you the wampum which we received from you when you suffered loss by death. We now conclude our speeches. Now show us the man whom we are to proclaim as Chief in place of the deceased.

Condolence Belt

This belt was used in the mourning ceremonies for a Chief (Hoyaneh). The two diamonds signifies the opposite Brother or Sisterhoods, one of which mourned and one of which condoled. The V-shaped design represents the chief's antlers, his title or symbol of chieftainship.

It is provided thus: If the Three Elder Brothers (Mohawk, Onondaga, Seneca) shall lose one of their chiefs by death, the Younger Brothers (Cayuga, Tuscarora, Oneida) shall come to the surviving chiefs of the Three Brothers on the tenth day and console them. If the Younger brothers lose one of their chiefs, then the Three Elder Brothers shall on the tenth day come to them and console them. The consolation shall be the reading of the contents of the thirteen wampum strings of Ayonwhatha. At the termination of this rite, a successor shall be appointed by the women heirs of the chieftainship title. When the women title holders shall have chosen one of their sons, the chiefs of the League will assemble in two places, the Younger Brothers in one place and the Older Brothers in another. The chiefs who are to console the mourning chiefs shall choose one of their number to sing the Song Of Peace as they journey to the sorrowing chiefs. The singer shall lead the way, and the chiefs and the people shall follow. When they reach the sorrowing chiefs, they shall hail the candidate chief and will then perform the rite of conferring the chieftainship title.

It is provided thus: When a candidate chief is to be installed, he shall furnish four wampum strings, one span in length, bound together at one end. Such will be his pledge to the chiefs of the League that he will live according to the Constitution of the Great Peace and that he will exercise justice in all affairs. When the pledge is finished, the speaker of the council must hold the wampum strings in his hand and address the opposite side of the Council Fire. He shall begin the address saying, "Now behold him. He has now become a chief of the League. See how splendid he looks." An address may then follow. At the end of it, he sends the wampum to the opposite side, and it shall be received as evidence of the pledge. Then shall the opposite side

Kathy Montour with Condolence Belt.

say, "We now crown you with the sacred emblem of the deer's antlers, the emblem of your chieftainship. You shall now become a mentor of the people of the Five Nations. The thickness of your skin shall be seven spans, which is to say that you shall be proof against anger, offensive actions, and criticism. Your heart shall be filled with peace and good will. Your mind shall be filled with a yearning for the welfare of the people of the League. With endless patience you shall carry out your duty, and your firmness shall be tempered with tenderness for your people. Neither anger nor fury shall find lodging in your mind. All of your words and actions shall be marked with calm deliberation. In all of your deliberations in the Council of the League, in your efforts at law making, in all of your official acts, self interests shall be cast away. Do not cast over your shoulder behind you the warning of your nephews and nieces (your people) should they chide you for any error or wrong you may do, but return to the way of the Great Law which is right and just. Look and listen for the welfare of the whole people, and have always in view not only the present, but also the coming generations, even those whose faces are yet beneath the surface of the ground—the unborn of the future nation."

Adoption

It is provided thus: The father of a child of great comeliness, learning, ability or specially loved because of some circumstances may, at the will of the child's clan select a name from his own (the father's) clan and bestow it by ceremony, such as is provided. This

Don Fadden holding Adoption pledge wampum string.

name shall be only temporary, and shall be called "a name hung about the neck."

It is provided thus: Should any person, a member of the League of Five Nations, especially esteem a man or a woman of another clan or of a foreign nation, he may choose a name and bestow it upon that person so esteemed. The naming shall be in accord with the ceremony of bestowing names. Such a name is only temporary and shall be called "a name hung about the neck." A short string of wampum shall be delivered with the name as a record and a pledge.

It is provided thus: Should any member of the Five Nations, a family, or a person belonging to a foreign nation submit a proposal for adoption into a clan of one of the Five Nations, he or they shall furnish a string of wampum, a span in length, as a pledge to the clan into which he or they wish to be adopted. The Chiefs of the nation shall then consider the proposal and submit a decision.

It is provided thus: Any member of the Five Nations, who through esteem or other feelings, wishes to adopt an individual, a family, or a number of families may offer adoption to him or them, and if accepted, the matter shall be brought to the attention of the Chiefs for confirmation and the Chiefs must confirm in the adoption.

It is provided thus: When the adoption of anyone shall have been confirmed by the Chiefs of the nation, the Chiefs shall address the people of the nation and say, "Now you of our nation be informed that _____ (such a person, such a family, or such families) have ceased forever to bear their birth nation's name and have buried it in the depth of the earth. Henceforth let no one of our nation ever mention the original name or nation of their birth. To do so will hasten the end of our peace."

Emigration Belt

It is provided thus: When a person or family belonging to the Five Nations desires to abandon their nation and the territory of the Five Nations, they shall inform the chiefs of their nation and the Council of the League of Five Nations shall take notice of it. When any person or any of the people of the Five Nations emigrate and reside in a distant region away from the territory of the League of Five Nations, the Chiefs of the Five Nations at will may send a messenger carrying a broad belt of black wampum. When the messenger arrives, he shall call the people together or address them personally, displaying the belt of black wampum, and they shall know that this is an order for them to return to their original homes and to their council fire.

Dan Thompson holding Emigration Belt.

The Coming of The People with White Faces—A Record Belt

This belt records the condition of the early white people who came to the Iroquois Country. The strong outside diagonal lines supporting the weak inside diagonal line represents the Five Nations, the Iroquois. The thin, weak inside line represents the early whites. The Indians supported these early whites, holding them up so that they would not fall down, that is, showing them how to hunt, to farm, and teaching them how to survive and live in this country until they were strong enough to support themselves. When these early white people were cold, hungry, (and it happened often) and their little ones cried for bread, it was the Indian who gave them meat, corn, and fish. When rival whites and their allies attempted to invade these early English Dutch and Swedish settlers, it was the Iroquois who stood in the trail and blocked their way.

Coming of the White Faces Belt held by Glenn Young.

Two-Row Wampum

This belt symbolizes the agreement and conditions under which the Iroquois welcomed the white peoples to this land "You say that you are our Father and I am your son." We say, "We will not be like Father and Son, but like Brothers. This wampum belt confirms our

Connie Jock holding
Two-Row Wampum Belt.

words. These two rows will symbolize two paths or two vessels, traveling down the same river together. One, a birch bark canoe, will be for the Indian People, their laws, their customs, and their ways. The other, a ship, will be for the white people and their laws, their customs, and their ways. We shall each travel the river together, side by side, but in our own boat. Neither of us will make compulsory laws or interfere in the internal affairs of the other. Neither of us will try to steer the other's vessel."

The Two-Row Wampum agreement has been kept by the Iroquois to this date.

Glenn Jock holding Champlain Wampum Belt.

Champlain—A Record Belt

French Invasion—This belt was made to keep in memory the expeditions of the French against the Five Nations. The Iroquois never forgave (and the French would never let them forget) the French of Canada for invading their territory and killing and torturing their people, as well as burning their villages. Champlain was the first offender and De Nonville the last to do serious injury. Up until twenty-four years after Champlain had killed three Mohawk men at Lake Champlain, the Iroquois had not tried to kill any Frenchmen, though many of their own people had been murdered by the French. They tried in vain to use reason with the invading whites but when pressed beyond endurance, they turned on the French and time after time defeated them and their allies. There is plenty of documentary evidence that it was the Iroquois, not the English, who defeated the French in the so-called French and Indian Wars. One noted historian said that when the English colonies outnumbered the Iroquois five to one that they were still begging the Iroquois for protection and they were receiving it.

Two choices faced by the French, war or the white wampum of peace.

Huron Alliance Belt

After the Hurons were conquered by the Five Nations in 1650, many were taken in by the Iroquois. Whole villages were adopted by the Senecas and Mohawks. This belt became a Seneca belt and was taken to Grand River Lands (Ohsweken) after the American revolution. Its meaning is lost.

To read the history of the Hurons written by non-Indians one is led to believe that all of the Hurons were massacred by the Five Nations, that none were given any quarter, that all died at the stake, etc. These stories of the savagery and cruelties of the Iroquois were especially spread by the Jesuit missionaries. These early missionaries were a people convinced that they had a special monopoly on revealed truth, at least of such "truth" as they alone were prepared to recognize. Their accounts of Iroquois tortures, almost always second or third hand, are told with the usual zest for horror that was not actually witnessed by the writer. These early writers had a keen nose for terror stories about the "heathen" Indians, especially the Iroquois, whom they could not conquer. The horror detailed in their tales strangely read like the accounts of European tortures practiced by their own people, including those inflicted by their church. Perhaps the words of a modern historian, Harry Dever of Cedarville, Michigan, will throw a little light on this subject. He says:

"Our historians have done the Iroquois a great injustice. Canadian and American historians have been unanimous in showing the Iroquois as a bunch of blood thirsty fiends who ravaged the far north, northwest, and west. Through a by far more thorough study of the voluminous Jesuit Relations than has probably been made before I have discovered that for the latter two thirds of the seventeenth century the French cruelly libeled the Iroquois, that the Iroquois had to stay pretty close to northern New York State to protect themselves against a ring of troublesome neighbors, including the Mohicans, the Conestogas, the Eries, the Neutrals, the Hurons, the Montagnais, and especially the French, who were the instigators of all of their friction with the Iroquois. The French invented a lot of Iroquois atrocities to excuse to the English their intention to take over the Iroquois territory, which they correctly considered superior to Quebec. Every time they attempted to do so of course the Iroquois clobbered them. The only authentic Iroquois "atrocity" was the so-called LaChine Massacre, which was in retaliation for a far worse act of treachery by the French.

All of the other "atrocities," including the purported destruction of the Hurons, rested entirely on the imagination of French propagandists. The Hurons were largely destroyed by famine and disease, and most of the survivors joined the Iroquois, from whom they could expect the utmost generosity all Indians extended the starving no matter how ill-fed they were themselves.

The truth of it is that the Jesuits had become so hated by the Hurons that their lives were no longer safe outside of their fort at Ste. Marie. Yes, only toward the end did the Jesuit Superior admit that what for years he had been calling a "residence" was really a fort, garrisoned by French soldiers. The Jesuit Superior had to explain why they were abandoning all of their factitious Huron converts, and

Huron Belt shown by Roger Jock.

conceived the brilliant idea of reporting them massacred by the Iroquois. Most of our naive historians have made fools of themselves by swallowing French propaganda that has misled most of our historians for two or three centuries. I can assure you that I can substantiate my statements by quotations from the Jesuit Relations and other 17th century sources, of which I have a plethora. This gross injustice to the memory of the old Iroquois should be corrected."

The following recorded statement of an early French governor reveals just how the Iroquois were regarded in those days: (*Memoir of M. De La Barre, Quebec, Oct. 1, 1684*) "RESOLUTION: First, to endeavor to divide the Iroquois among themselves, and for this purpose to send persons expressly to communicate my sentiments to the Reverend Jesuit Fathers who are missionaries there and to request them to act." (Paris Document II).

The founders of the Great Peace did not intend that it include the Five Nations alone. The great Tree of Peace had branches large enough to include all of mankind. All Indian peoples, including the Hurons, were invited to sit beneath its branches. The following words of one of the Iroquois speakers inviting the Hurons to become members of the Iroquois Confederacy has been recorded: "Brothers, with this wampum belt I deliver a message from the Five Nations, assembled at their Council Fire at Onondaga Hill. They recommend that we be friends. They advise you not to listen to any bad reports, not to anything that would disturb your minds. Onondiio (French Governor) has sent evil birds among you. They speak with forked tongues. Onondiio would not like to see us live together as brothers."

Pat Jock holding First William Penn Belt.

First William Penn Belt

This belt was given to the Indians before they entered the Council House where the treaty was to be made. It was a token of amity and good faith. The figure with the white heart represents the white man and the other figure represents the Indian. When the treaty had been concluded and the Indians went out of the Council House with William Penn, they presented him with a return belt as evidence of their good faith. As usual, the treaty was faithfully kept by the Indians but was broken by Penn's sons after their father died and they gained power.

Mark Jock with William Penn Belt.

William Penn Belt

This is the original belt delivered by the Lenni-Lenape (Delaware) Chiefs to William Penn at the celebrated peace treaty under the elm tree at Shackamaxon in 1682. The hand of William Penn is joined in friendship with the hand of the Indian, and the two smokes (councils) of the two peoples are joined together as one. William Penn at that time said these words to the Indians, "We meet on the broad pathway of good faith and good will. No advantage shall be taken on either side, but all shall be openness and love. We are the same as if one man's body was to be divided into two parts. We are of one flesh and blood." The reply of the Lenni-Lenape Chief was as follows, "We will live in love with William Penn and his children as long as the creeks and rivers run, and while the sun, moon, and stars endure."

Penobscot-Onondaga Belt

Many people think, including many Indian people, that the Iroquois Confederacy was formed for the exclusive benefit of only the original Five Nations, that all other people were excluded from the Kayenerenhkowa, the Great Peace Law. This is not true. We have records of at least thirty-nine Indian peoples who took shelter beneath The Tree of Peace, most of them eventually becoming members or citizens of the Iroquois Confederacy.

The Peacemaker's thoughts had not been for Iroquois-speaking peoples alone but included all of mankind, and it was not by force alone that the Confederacy held the vast region under their peace. Reason, honesty, statesmanship, justice, and a keen knowledge of peace itself made it a success. The Peacemaker's great mind intended that under the shelter of The Tree of Peace all nations of mankind could rest. He, the Law Giver, said, "Hold fast to friends, for in union there is strength. Welcome the stranger and give him shelter, for he may become a prop to your house. Bury your hates and let them be forgotten, for if old stories are to be revived there can never be an end to war. Let us have one mind, one heart, one soul, in which all of the nations of the world shall be contained. We will have one head, one spirit, one blood, and we will speak with one tongue."

Throughout their history the Iroquois have sought, and still seek, to add braces to their Long House. Today, many Indian peoples, other than Iroquois, are seen at the councils and festivals of the Confederacy. When the Confederacy was new, the Tuscaroras, Creeks, Cherokees, Catawba, Nanticoke, Tutelo, Shawnee, Delaware, and scores of other southern peoples were approached by Iroquois runners carrying invitation wampum to council with the Confederacy. They also penetrated the forests to the Wabanaki Peoples to the east, the Passamaquody, Micmac, Penobscot, Maliseet, and others. Nations to the westward, the Miamis, Osage, Ojibway, Tobacco Nation, Huron, Ottawas, Sacs, Foxes, Eries, and others received the runners carrying the invitation wampum. The Confederacy received embassies from the peoples of Nova Scotia. Iroquois runners even penetrated to Mexico,

Andrea Boots holding Penobscot-Onondaga Belt.

and traditions say that they brought back seeds and tropical plants. From nation to nation the messengers of the Great Peace went carrying invitation wampum, inviting representatives to sit beneath the Tree of Peace and to talk over the advantages of an alliance. Most of

Onondaga, People of the Hills.

these distant nations sent two of their wisest men as representatives to the Great Council. Later, the Iroquois long had hopes that they might bring both the English and the French under the Great Tree. But at the time, it was beyond their reasoning. Only in recent time, through the United Nations, has the mind of white men tried to reach up to the brilliant reasoning and thoughts of the great Indian Peacemaker.

If reason and peaceful methods failed to change the mind of a military nation, they were warned three times in open council to obey the Great Law and settle their disagreements by reason rather than by force. If, after the third warning, the hostile people still insisted upon force to gain their ends, they were attacked by the Iroquois and the war continued until that nation was conquered. When a foreign nation was conquered or by its own will accepted The Great Peace, the war stopped immediately. The conquered people were not all tortured nor did they become slaves of the Iroquois. (Iroquois laws were against slavery.) They were taken in and adopted, and they became members of the nation who adopted them. They became equally esteemed by the Iroquois who regarded them as their own people. In fact, many of them in time became noted members and leaders of the Iroquois. If the defeated people chose to remain in their own territory, they were allowed to do so, and they could also keep their own system of internal government. However, they must cease all strife with other nations. The Confederacy protected the nations which they had conquered from hostile nations and also from white settlers. Weaker peoples, who asked permission, were often moved nearer to the heart of the Confederacy, who sent strong young warriors to see that they were not harmed by invaders of their settlements.

Iroquois territory, especially after the white man came, became the great asylum of many Indian peoples. It became a great "melting pot" of dispossessed Indian peoples. A system of unity of peoples was created which would have been impossible under any European system. The lands under the Confederacy covered many thousand square miles. In fact, the territory possessed by The Iroquois Nation was greater in extent than that of the boasted Empire of Rome at its greatest height.

The Penobscot-Onondaga belt is a friendship belt, an invitation sent from the Capital of the Iroquois Confederacy, Onondaga, to the Penobscot Nation, an invitation summons to attend a Condolence Council at Onondaga.

It is provided thus: Roots have spread out from the Tree of The Great Peace, one to the north, one to the east, one to the south, and one to the west. These are the Great White Roots, and their nature is peace and strength. If any man or any nation outside of the Five Nations shall obey the Laws of The Great Peace (Kaianerekowa), and shall make this known to the statesmen of the League, they may trace back the roots to the Tree. If their minds are clean, and if they are obedient and promise to obey the wishes of the Council of the League, they shall be welcomed to take shelter beneath the Tree of the Long Leaves.

Grade school student Angela Swamp holds the
Iroquois-Ojibway Friendship Belt.

Iroquois-Ojibway Friendship Belt

This belt is a friendship belt, and the symbols on the belt represent two nations joined together by the Path of Peace. One square
represents the Ojibway Nation and the other square represents the
Iroquois. There will always be an open path between them.

Kathy and Wendy Montour holding Invitation Belt.

Invitation to Enter
The Confederacy Belt

It is provided thus: That a belt of black wampum, nine rows in width, with four short white strands at each end, and having five hexagonal designs, shall represent the combined territory of the Five Confederate Nations in which each one of the hexagonal designs shall denote the separate territory of each of the Five Confederate Nations (Mohawk, Oneida, Onondaga, Cayuga, Seneca). The four short white strands at each end represent the sacred White Roots of the Tree of Peace or the Doorways of the Great Peace, wide open to alien nations to enter and receive the policy of the Great Peace and to abandon hostilities, to settle difficulties and disagreements by council rather than by blood and war.

Dan Thompson holding belt commemorating
"When Tuscaroras were taken in."

Tuscarora Taken In Belt

This belt has been called the Six Nations Brace Belt and records when the Tuscarora Nation was taken into the Iroquois Confederacy. Each diagonal band represents a state or nation of the Confederacy, a brace or supporting beam of The Long House, by which the Iroquois often called their league. The braces represent an alliance for purposes of peace. This belt commemorates the admission of the Tuscaroras to take shelter under The Tree Of Peace, the Iroquois United Nations.

Six Nations Peace Belt

It is provided thus: It shall be the duty of all of the chiefs of The Great Law Of Peace or the Longhouse People from time to time, as occasion demands, to act as teachers and spiritual guides of their people and remind them of their Creator's will and words. They shall say,

"Listen that peace may continue unto future days!

Always listen to the words of the Great Creator, for he has spoken.

United People, let not evil find lodging in your minds,

For the Great Creator has spoken and the cause of peace shall not become old.

The cause of peace shall not die if you remember the Great Creator."

It is provided thus: When a member of an alien nation comes to the territory of the Great Peace League and seeks refuge and permanent residence, the statesmen of the nation to which he comes shall extend hospitality and make him a member of the nation. Then shall he be accorded equal rights and privileges in all matters as long as he obeys the laws of the Great Peace.

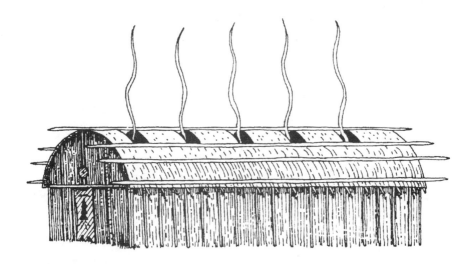

Andy Swamp holding Six Nations Peace Belt.

This belt is a peace belt, and the white wampum in the belt stands for peace. The six diamonds woven into the belt stand for the territory and council fires of the Six Nations, the Mohawks, Oneidas, Onondagas, Cayugas, Tuscaroras, and Senecas.

Belt of the Six Nations

Nelson Jock holding return of the Tuscaroras belt.

This belt announced the return of the nomadic Tuscaroras, and it was made in 1714. The Six Nations are represented by purple-colored, step-like triangle designs. For the first time it gives official recognition to the white man in Indian affairs, the symbol of the invader being indicated in the lower corner.

Tuscarora, People of the Shirt.

Carla Laughingwaters holding Council Fire Belt.

Council Fire of
Six Nations Belt

This belt means that the Iroquois are a united people, that the Path of Peace connects their territories, their Council Fires (Governments). Wampum belts are historical documents commemorating significant events in Iroquois life.

Oneida Tribal Belt

This belt was long in the possession of Chief Skenando of the Oneidas, the friend and ally of George Washington during the Revolutionary War period. The belt was known as the Tribal Belt of the

Oneida Tribal Belt held by Glenn Jock.

Oneida Nation. The six squares represent the territories of the Six Nations: the Mohawks, Oneidas, Onondagas, Cayugas, Tuscaroras and Senecas, who are joined together as one people, one nation, one country. The six diamonds are the council fires of each state of the six united brothers.

One time Skenando was on an official trip to Albany. While there, his so-called "friends" fed him liquor until he passed out unconscious. When he awoke, he found himself with his face in the gutter, all of his ceremonial clothing and possessions gone. He vowed never to drink the white man's firewater again. When he returned home, he said to his people, "Drink no firewater of the white man. It makes you

Oneida, People of Standing Stone.

mice for the white men who are cats. Many a meal they have eaten of you." The old Oneida who held this fine belt died at Oneida Village at the age of 110 years. Just before his death, he said these words to his people, "I am like an aged hemlock. The winds of a hundred winters have whistled through my branches. I am dead at the top. The generation to which I belong have gone away and left me. Why I live, the Great Spirit only knows."

Iroquois Territory
Wampum Strings

It is provided thus: A bunch of wampum strings is to be the symbol of the Council Fire of the League of Six Nations. The chief whom the Council of Firekeepers (Onondaga) shall appoint to speak for them in opening the Council shall hold the strings of shells in his hands when speaking. When he finishes speaking, he shall place the strings on an elevated place or pole so that all the assembled Chiefs and the people may see it and know that the Council is open and in progress. These six strings of wampum tied together as one shall represent the Six Nations. Each sting shall represent one territory, and the whole a completely united territory known as The Six Nations Territory.

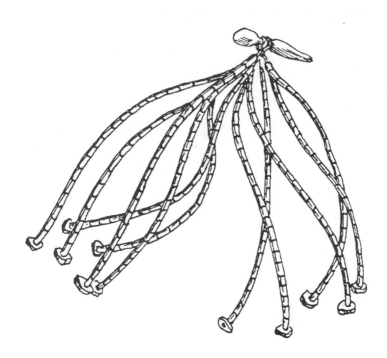

Don Fadden holding Iroquois Territory wampum strings.

Roger Jock holding friendship belt.

Great Britain and Six Nations Friendship Belt

The Keeper of the Wampum was thoroughly versed in the interpretation of the wampum records, and once or twice a year he took the belts and wampum strings and recited their meanings to the public—for use in ritual and ceremony, white indicated peace, health, and good will, while purple indicated sorrow, death, and mourning. A string composed entirely of purple wampum was sent by one nation to the chiefs of a related nation to notify them of the death of a chief. A white wampum string painted red was sent as a declaration of war. A belt having a hatchet designed on it and painted red was sent with a bag or roll of tobacco to a nation as an invitation to join in war. Belts were employed for official communication and for summoning councils. The selected delegates from other nations presented belts or strings as their credentials. At the opening of a council, an address was made to the representatives from each nation in turn and a belt given them which they preserved as a substitute for a written record. Belts were used also for the ratification of treaties and the confirmation of alliances. This belt is a treaty belt and expresses friendship. The squares represent two nations, the Iroquois and the British. The dark square in the center of the wider square represents their council Fire or government. The purple line connecting the squares represents the friendly pathway between them. Roads from one friendly nation to another are generally marked by one or two rows of wampum running through the middle of the belt from end to end. It means that they keep up friendly intercourse with each other.

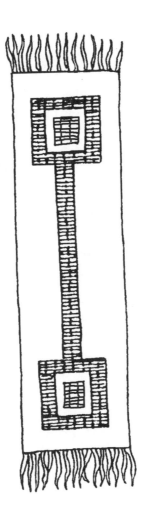

*Delaware Land Belt held (from left to right) by Pat Jock,
Tina Big Bear Anderson, and Cindy Boots.*

Delaware Land Belt

This belt records the conditions under which the Lenni-Lenape or Delaware Nation ceded a certain tract of their territory to the white man, and that they retained the right to travel, hunt and fish on the lands parted with, the design representing their trail to and fro over the territory sold.

Sir William Johnson Dish Belt

This belt is called the Sir William Johnson Dish Belt by its owner. It was supposed to have been sent by Sir William Johnson, colonial Indian agent of England for northern Indians, to Indian allies of Canada. It was to notify the friendly nations of the English, who were fighting the French, of the existence of food and supplies at four points, Fort Stanwix, Niagara, Oswego, etc.

Edgar Jock holding Sir William Johnson Belt.

Defeat of the French Record Belt

This is an Onondaga belt and was made as a record. A French priest who was stationed at Onondaga told a French boy captive of the Onondagas that a French army was to invade the Iroquois Country, starting with the Onondagas. He, the priest, was secretly storing gun power and other military supplies in a small house in back of the mission, supplies that he received from time to time from French traders who visited Onondaga. The boy who had lived with the Onondagas and who was adopted by them, liked their ways, and considered himself an Onondaga, told the Chiefs. The Onondagas then demanded to see the inside of the little building behind the mission. The priest refused, saying that the log building was a holy place, that only he could enter. They forced their way in and found that the boy's story was true. They killed the black robe and renounced Catholicism. They met the French army and defeated it. The belt was made as a record of the event so that they would not be taken in again, fooled by words. The cross at the top of the belt represents French Canada. The long line to the figure of the man is the trail of the priest from Canada. The human figure is the priest and the diamond-shaped design at the bottom represents Onondaga.

Onondaga, Hill People.

Jake Swamp's son, Andy Swamp,
holding Onondaga record belt.

Governor Denny's Invitation Belt

This wampum belt was sent by Governor Denny of the Pennsylvania Province to the Indians, especially the Delaware and Shawnee People of the Ohio Region, to attend a peace and alliance council at Philadelphia. The Governor was very anxious to secure the fighting ability of Indians to use against the French who, the same as the English, had their eyes on the rich Ohio Region. During the wars in Europe between the French and the English, these two nations spared no effort to get different Indian nations in America to fight against their rivals in the "New World." Both the French and the English desired the fur trade of the Iroquois and other Indian nations. Both the French and English cast greedy eyes on the lands of the Indians. Both claimed the Iroquois Country as their own. The Iroquois never admitted that either the French or the English had any claim over them or their country. The following is part of a speech of the Iroquois spokesman to Governor Fletcher of Albany concerning this: "You say that we are subjects to the King of England and the Duke of York. We say that we are brethren, and take care of ourselves." When English representatives tried to prevent the Iroquois from meeting with the French, the Iroquois speaker informed the English thus:

"The privilege of meeting in general council when we please is a privilege we always have enjoyed. No former governor of the name of Corlear (name of every governor of the Province of New York) ever obstructed this privilege. We planted a Tree of Peace in this place with them. Its roots and branches extend as far as Virginia and New England, and we have reposed with pleasure under its shade. Brother, let us keep to that first tree, and let us be untied and unanimous. Such prohibition of our assemblies will be of ill consequences, and occasion differences between us."

Needless to say, New York Colony was wise to see that they had better agree with the Onondaga speaker and let the matter rest if they valued their own safety and the protection of the Iroquois against the French.

Barry Montour holding Governor Denny's Invitation Belt.

All English governors encouraged the Iroquois and their followers to attack the French and their allies. The French likewise encouraged the Hurons, Eries, Susquehannocks, and other Indian nations to attack the English and the Iroquois. The unfortunate Iroquois, whose Confederacy had been formed to bring about peace among all people, tried in vain to get the French and the English to cease warfare and invited them to take shelter beneath their Tree of Peace. Their efforts were wasted. Indian peoples living between these two rival white colonies realized that they were being used as tools, and in all of the wars between the warlike Europeans, they—the Indian—were the main ones to suffer. Both sides made many promises to the Indians for their aid, promises which neither European nation kept after the war was over and the aid of the Indians was no longer needed.

Governor Denny's belt was one of many such belts sent to Indians asking for their aid in fighting rival white colonies.

Caughnawaga—Oka—St. Regis Belt

This belt is sometimes called the Seven Nations Belt. It is a record belt, that is, it records a happening. It means this:

Their path is not straight. They have forsaken the Great Law and gone to the land of the cross, Canada. This belt represents the union of the Seven Nations, and the crooked line at the bottom represents that they were crooked (Roman Catholic). This particular belt embodies the pledge of the seven Canadian Christianized nations to abandon their crooked ways and to keep an honest peace. It was given to the Five Nations by the Seven Nations to mark their submission to the power of the Iroquois Confederacy, with a promise of peace. The Seven Nations, organized and encouraged by French Catholic priests, was a political union of parts of certain settlements of Iroquois and Algonquins whom the Catholic missionaries had christianized and influenced. The settlements that made up the so-called Seven Nations were as follows: Mohawk Band at Lake of Two Mountains, Algonquin Band at Lake of Two Mountains, Nipissing Band at Lake of Two Mountains, part of Caughnawaga Band, Oswegatchie Band (near Ogdensburg, N.Y.), Hurons of Lorett, and Abenakis of St. Francis. When the Oswegatchies were scattered by the whites, the priests said that St. Regis would take their place.

Andrea Boots holding Seven Nations Belt.

Wolf Belt

Angela Swamp with Akwesasne Wolf Belt.

This belt was an Akwesasne or St. Regis Belt and once belonged to Chief Running Deer of the Akwesasne Mohawks. The center figures, two men, represent the French and Praying Indians (Caughnawaga, St. Regis, Oka and their allies) clasping their hands in friendship. The seven purple lines signify what is called the Seven Nations. The color between the seven black lines is white and means a peace path. This is guarded at each end, east and west, by the Wolf Clan, symbolized by the purple colored animal figures. The heredity Keeper of the Eastern Door of the Long House was of the Wolf Clan and the Western Doorkeeper (Seneca) was also of the Wolf Clan. The Mohawks traded with the French but were never in their alliance.

Three generations of Wolf Clan women.

Revolutionary War
Two Road Belt

At the beginning of the Revolutionary War the Iroquois tried to remain neutral, but it did not take them long to realize that neither the English or the Americans intended to leave their country out of the war. One Indian compared his people to a piece of cloth between a pair of scissors, the scissors being the contesting white people and the Indians being the cloth that was cut. Such was to be the case, and it was not the first or the twentieth time that the Indian found himself in that position. England used every method to incite the Iroquois against the Americans, and the United States did not hesitate then, or in all of her wars, to use Indians to fight her battles. Both sides made many promises to the Indians for their aid, promises which neither white nation kept after the war was over and the aid of the Indians was no longer needed. Both sides offered scalp bounties, but the English went a little farther; they offered a larger reward for scalps than they did for prisoners, thus making killing more profitable. As the war progressed the Iroquois found themselves in a very trying position. Pressure from both groups was put on them. At a great council at Onondaga, the Capital of the Six Nations, they talked over the problem. Some were for helping Great Britain because of the ancient Treaty of Friendship and alliance made with her so many years before. Besides, had not the Americans broken the Treaty of Forth Stanwix and crowded them from their lands? England promised them that in case Great Britain lost the war, the Six Nations would be given an amount of land in Canada equal to that lost in their present country. The Oneidas and Tuscaroras, members of the Iroquois League, did not want to fight the Americans due to the influence of Reverend Samuel Kirkland and the Christian New England Indians who had settled in their country. The white man had not yet reached their lands and crowded them off as they had done the Mohawks. You must remember that in order for the Iroquois to officially declare war, it was necessary for each state in their union to declare war. According to the Iroquois Constitution it had to be unanimous. Council after council was held but all could not agree as to what policy to follow. The Mohawks were for war. The Onondagas were neutral. The Senecas and Cayugas were lukewarm to either side. The Oneidas and Tuscaroras sympathized with the struggling colonies.

Cindy Boots displays Two Road Belt.

Even within a nation all could not agree. Finally Thayendinagea, a Mohawk war leader, said, "Let each nation be responsible for its own members. Let each nation decide for itself what path it will take in this war." He held up this wampum belt, which has on it the figures of two roads. They represent the road of the English and the road of the American colonies. The nations of the Iroquois could choose either road to follow. This belt, as well as the war, did harm to the Iroquois and helped to divide them.

George Washington Belt

This belt, called the George Washington Belt, is a covenant belt with the thirteen original United States. The thirteen large figures of men represent the thirteen states, their hands joined in friendship with the two center figures who are standing at each side of a house. The two center men are the Mohawks (Keepers of the Eastern Door of the Long House or Iroquois Confederacy) and the Senecas (Keeper or Door-keeper of the western part of the League). This belt commemorates the Treaty of Peace made during Washington's presidency. Among promises made by the United States in this treaty was that the United States acknowledged the lands reserved to the Six Nations to be the property of the Six Nations and that the United States would never disturb or claim these lands, that the lands were to remain theirs until they chose to sell the same to the United States, who alone had the right to purchase. The United States also promised that they would protect the Six Nations from any (outside alien force), including separate states, and that it would not interfere nor

Dave Jock holding George Washington Belt.

let anyone else interfere in the internal affairs of the Six Nations. The Six Nations, in their usual Indian way, held the treaty inviolate. Had the white man honored this treaty, all western New York State would be owned by the Iroquois. In token of this treaty, the United States still gives certain Iroquois three or four yards of calico cloth each autumn. The Iroquois today live in hopes that the white citizens of the state and nation will see that the promises of justice and fair play promised in this treaty will be carried out. They, themselves, have kept faith for over 200 years.

Dan Thompson holding Fort Stanwix Treaty Belt.

Fort Stanwix Treaty Belt

This belt was exchanged at the signing of the Treaty between the Six Nations and the United States at Fort Stanwix (Rome, N.Y.) Oct. 22, 1784. At this treaty (as in all others) the Six Nations was guaranteed the right of occupancy forever in the immemorial domain of the Iroquois League. The United States further promised to prevent anyone, including any state, from taking Indian lands or from interfering in the internal affairs of the Six Nations. As usual, the Six Nations alone faithfully kept the agreements made at this treaty.

Confessional Wampum of Handsome Lake, The Seneca Prophet and Teacher

This wampum is ten strings, all white, all pure and sacred, held in the hands of the followers of the Prophet while confessing sins before the Creator, and pledging to try in the future to lead a better and more pure life.

In 1735 at the Seneca town of Conawagus on the Genesee River, there was born an Indian boy who was later to become one of the greatest Indian prophets and teachers of recent times. This Seneca was later given the office of a Chief of the Turtle Clan with the title of Kaniatario, or Handsome Lake.

As a a young man, Handsome Lake was everything but a religious teacher. He was an habitual drinker of the white man's firewater and more than once returned from the towns of the invader under the influence of the white man's curse. At this time, in spite of the promises of the United States Government to keep the fur traders from bringing rum into Indian towns and despite the warnings of the Confederate Chiefs to these same traders, liquor was circulated freely among the Iroquois. The Senecas, who had lost most of their beautiful country and who were becoming more and more surrounded by the whites, sought to forget their troubles by drinking rum. Under such conditions Handsome Lake lived.

Finally, after years of drinking, Handsome Lake became very ill— so ill, that for four years he lay an invalid, not able to rise from his bed. At the time of the fourth year, he walked from his cabin and fell to the earth, seemingly dead. His daughter immediately told his clan relatives of his death. His body was dressed in his ceremonial clothes and he was prepared for burial. When his relatives gathered for the Death Ceremony, he surprised everyone by sitting up, or as his followers say, "Came to life."

From that day on, Handsome Lake was a teacher and a prophet. Three Messengers of the Great Spirit had come to him during his

Roger Jock holds panel upon which
Confessional Wampum is mounted.

death. They told him that the Creator of Mankind had chosen him to tell the Iroquois People how they should live and worship. From time to time for the next fifteen years, the Three Messengers visited and instructed Handsome Lake with the wishes of the Creator. At such times, Handsome Lake would go into a deep trance. There was a fourth Messenger who was to come when the Prophet was to leave the earth at the time of death.

His most important message was to condemn the use of the white man's firewater. He said that it was for the white man's use only and not for the Indian, that it was sent over to America by the Evil Spirit to destroy the Indian.

Handsome Lake checked this curse of the white man and thus saved the Indian from eventual extermination. His influence against the drink habit was very noticeable among the Iroquois. It attracted the attention of neighboring white people. President Thomas Jefferson wrote the Chiefs of the Six Nations a letter, praising the teachings of Handsome Lake and advising the Iroquois to follow his teachings.

The prophet taught that to be poor was no disgrace, that those who are poor on earth will have plenty in the Spirit World. He said that those who imitated the invader and became rich in worldly possessions, thus forgetting to share with the less fortunate, were bought by the Evil Spirit. He said it was impossible for a rich man to enter the Spirit World.

Handsome Lake urged the Iroquois to follow Indian customs and ways, that the ancient ceremonies of Iroquois thanking the Creator for his many gifts pleased the Creator.

Handsome Lake taught that the really great man, one who was successful in this world, was not the man who gained for himself wealth and power, but was the man who did the most for his people.

He told the Council of Chiefs that in order to protect their country and people from the white man, it was necessary to send some of their most promising young people away to the white man's schools to learn the white man's own business methods and then return to the Indian Country to help their own nation. He said that unless they did this, they were doomed. These are only a few of the many lessons given by Sakoitison to the Three Messengers who in turn, passed them on to Handsome Lake to deliver to his people.

For sixteen years, Handsome Lake preached the religion, Kariwi-io. During that time, he preached at Cornplanter Reservation, Cold Spring Reservation, and Tonawanda Reservation. While at Tonawanda, he was visited by the Messengers of the Creator who told him that he was to go to Onondaga, and while there, the Fourth Messenger would come and lead Handsome Lake to the Land of Happy Spirits. His prediction of his own death was true; while at Onondaga, he died—August 10, 1815.

Alvin Jock and Edgar Jock holding Black Hawk belt.

A Black Hawk Belt

The Iroquois were not the only Indian people who used wampum belts. This belt was sent by Chief Black Hawk, the famous Sauk leader and patriot of the Indian nations at Traverse Bay, Michigan, with a message that their people should remain neutral during the campaigns and Indian revolts at Michilimackinac. Black Hawk had served under the great Shawnee leader, Tecumseh. The story of the life of this great leader, Black Hawk, is a sad one. He tried in vain to hold on to the little territory that his people had left, but it was sold from under him while he was absent. He said before his death these words:

"My reason teaches me that land cannot be sold. The Great Spirit gave it to his children to live upon. As long as they occupy and cultivate it, they have the right to the soil. Nothing can be sold but such things as can be carried away. The Earth is our Mother. Who among us has the right to sell his Mother? I love my country. I loved my towns and corn fields on the Rock River where I was born and where my Fathers lived before me. It was once a beautiful country and under its earth are the graves of my forefathers. It is sacred to me. I fought the white man that I might keep my country. I lost and now it is theirs. I charge them to respect it, to keep it as the Sauk did. I was once a great warrior, but now I am very poor. I love to look upon the Mississippi. I have looked upon it from childhood. I will always love that beautiful river. My home has always been upon its bank. We told them, the whites, to let us alone and keep away from us. But they followed on and beset our paths and they coiled themselves among us like snakes. They poisoned us by their touch. We are become like them, hypocrites and liars, adulterers and ladrones, all takers and no workers. The white man does not scalp the head (but they did). They do worse, they poison the heart. I have spoken."

Even in death Black Hawk was not allowed to rest. The following year white vandals invaded his sepulcher, cut off his head, took other parts of the skeleton, and attempted to put these grisly remains on exhibition in a tent show. Because of complaints of Black Hawk's sons, they were recovered again, where they were placed in the custody of the collections of the Burlington Geological and Historical Society. They were destroyed in 1855 when the building containing them was burned.

When The Akwesasne Mohawks Were Taken Back In Belt

This belt symbolizes the alliance of an adopted nation. This belt was made to record the time in 1885 when the Akwesasne (St. Regis) Mohawks were taken back into the Six Nations of the Iroquois Confederacy. The four lines represent rafters to strengthen the framework of a building (Long House). The Akwesasne Mohawks are as rafters to strengthen and act as a prop or brace to the Six Nations and by doing this, the Six Nations likewise act as rafters or a brace to prop up the Akwesasne Mohawks.

Belt commemorating return of the Mohawk Akwesasne to the League is held by Caroline Boots.

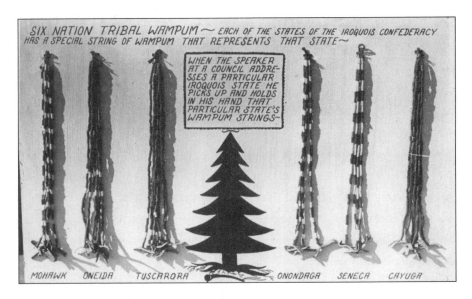

Unity Strings on display at the Six Nations Indian Museum in Onchiota, New York.

Six Nations Unity Strings

Six strings of purple wampum united at one end stand for the Six Nations. When this was laid in a circle the council was open. When it was taken up it meant that the council was over.

It is provided thus: A large bunch of wampum strings, in the making of which the Six Nations League Chiefs have equally contributed, shall symbolize the completeness of the Union and certify the pledge of the nations represented by the Chiefs of the League of the Mohawks, the Oneidas, the Onondagas, the Cayugas, the Tuscaroras, and the Senecas, that all are united and formed into one body, or union, called The Union Of The Great Law which they have established.

Don Fadden holding Six Nations Unity wampum strings.

An Unwilling Gift
From The Dead

This is a replica of a belt which was offered for sale in October, 1972, by collectors through a Park Avenue auction gallery. The original was dug up from a grave together with the bones of the children who were buried with it, probably within the last century in New York State.

White people who read this can rest fairly secure that when they die, their remains will not be disturbed. But Indian People find that the resting places of their grandmothers and grandfathers are fair play for archeologists—both professional and amateur—operating under the guise of "pursuit of knowledge." Even today Indian people worry that even in death they will be bothered and that their own bones may someday rest in a museum to be viewed by curious eyes.

Although the original meaning of this belt is not known to us, we display it here as a symbol of the persecution of Indian dead, and a sign of shame for those who do not know what "Rest in Peace" means.

Ancestors! Our Ancient Fathers and Mothers! We honor you and we will protect you!

Nelson Jock holds a Burial Belt.

Unknown belts held (from left to right) by Dan Thompson, Mike Jock, and Harold Edwards, Jr.

Unknown Belts

There are many, many wampum belts that we know of whose meanings have been lost. Some were bought from individual Indians who, in many cases, had no right to sell them. Many were stolen outright by trickery or force, sometimes by government officials who also had no right to seize them. Some were robbed from graves and placed in museums, and no one recalls their significance. The meaning of others has been lost as Indian communities have been disrupted by missionaries and government officials who have often encouraged Indian people to turn their backs on their own history and culture. In some cases educational officials, who should have known better, have also been guilty of this.

Wampum belts are in use today.

No one knows what the three belts shown in the photograph, a few of many such, mean. Their history and story is lost forever. Not only is this a loss to the Indian, but also it is a loss to non-Indians who are beginning to see the value of a beautiful heritage, Indian heritage, something which all people—Indian and non-Indian—can respect, enjoy, and share. These three belts are displayed as a reminder that unless we protect our culture and our people, we will incur a loss that will bring tears to the eyes of future generations.

These important Native American books
are available from your local bookstore.

Legends of the Iroquois by Tehanetorens
$9.95

Deer Dancer
$9.95

How Can One Sell the Air?
$6.95

Sacred Song of the Hermit Thrush by Tehanetorens
$5.95

Collecting Authentic Indian Arts & Crafts
$16.95